T0370477

Why Me?

WHY NOT ME!

Overcoming Tragedy, Addictions, and Challenges in Life.

Jon A. Logan

AuthorHouse™
1663 Liberty Drive
Bloomington, IN 47403
www.authorhouse.com
Phone: 1 (800) 839-8640

© 2015 Jon A. Logan. All rights reserved.

No part of this book may be reproduced, stored in a retrieval system,
or transmitted by any means without the written permission of the author.

Published by AuthorHouse 7/14/2015

ISBN: 978-1-5049-1955-5 (sc)
978-1-5049-1957-9 (hc)
978-1-5049-1956-2 (e)

Library of Congress Control Number: 2015910246

Print information available on the last page.

Any people depicted in stock imagery provided by Thinkstock are models,
and such images are being used for illustrative purposes only.
Certain stock imagery © Thinkstock.

This book is printed on acid-free paper.

Because of the dynamic nature of the Internet, any web addresses or links contained in this book may have changed
since publication and may no longer be valid. The views expressed in this work are solely those of the author and do
not necessarily reflect the views of the publisher, and the publisher hereby disclaims any responsibility for them.

This book is dedicated to anyone suffering in life. I want to thank my family Amy, Nicholas, and Brock for supporting me and providing the courage to share my story.

Life is what you make of it.

We have choices to make each day and I choose to wake up with a smile, tackle each challenge, and to look for new horizons to conquer. My renewed perspective has less to do with where I live or what I do, but rather, how I live each day. I did not always live my life with this attitude and I know there are others who have struggled with similar problems. It took me many years of doing the wrong things before I turned my life around. In this book I share my story with you, along with a few secrets for a happier, healthier life.

I was born in a small town hospital in northeast Nebraska, June 22, 1974. I grew up in a loving home, well-cared for by my parents and I knew I was on my way to a life of **"happily ever after."**

My father was a dentist and I felt lucky to have a stay-at-home mom for the first few years of my life. Our neighborhood was filled with other young families and lots of playmates. My older brother Mark had the most annoying tag along ever. **Guess who?** Our days were filled with football games, "Kick the Can" and "Ghost in the Graveyard". Since my dad was a bit of a pyromaniac, the Fourth of July was always special. The town was equally great for kids. We rode our bikes everywhere and frequented the local arcade with as many quarters as we could scrounge up. The scene may sound like fantasy but that is my perception; however I don't remember much of my childhood before age 9. I realize this seems odd and we will get to that shortly.

My mom was an intelligent woman who earned her master's degree in English. She put her career on hold to raise my brother and me. Mark, who is three years older, looks like my dad and I look more like Mom.

In old photo albums I see great times on vacations, old car shows, birthday parties, fun at Halloween and the excitement of many Christmases. I see myself, and the kids I grew up with, smiling and having fun.

Yet, when I view these memories,
I really don't feel happy emotions.

The first day of kindergarten I walked out and came home because

"I already knew what she was teaching".

The early years are scattered with tales of my independence. The first day of kindergarten I walked out of school and came home because "I already knew what she was teaching". I imagine this was the product of playing with flashcards instead of a dog. (Thank-you, Mom and Dad.) Education and preparation were important to my family. In my mind, however, preschool math and spelling were not better than a pet, even though I benefited in the long run.

On a trip to Busch Gardens at age four I wandered off causing my family panic until some nice lady, who spoke no English, took me by the hand to find my family. My father told me he thought the alligators had eaten me, (which I didn't think was possible), but it was funny to hear him tell the story. If you interviewed the parents of my early childhood friends you would find similar tales of me pushing or exceeding the limits.

Most people reading this would think, **what a lucky guy!**

By the time I was in elementary school my mother decided to use her degree for more than substitute teaching. She landed a job as a regional director for a large health organization focusing on education and preventing disease. My dad was extremely proud that she was in a career that provided professional satisfaction to her.

Be Thankful for
Every Day You Have

Dad, Mark and I set off for St. Louis to pick up my mom who was attending a conference. We were going on vacation to our nation's capital and picking her up on the way. We had one of those roomy Ford Econoline vans with two sets of captain chairs and a bench in back. The trip was as good as can be expected since we did not have electronic tablets, MP3 or DVD players of today's kids. I empathize with my parents because the

license plate game can only get you so far on a road trip. One morning after a tasty diner breakfast my dad decided to take a nap and let my mom do the driving. I was tired, too, so I slept in between the two captain chairs in the middle of the van (long before the restraint laws were in effect) and my brother Mark sat in the passenger chair in the front seat.

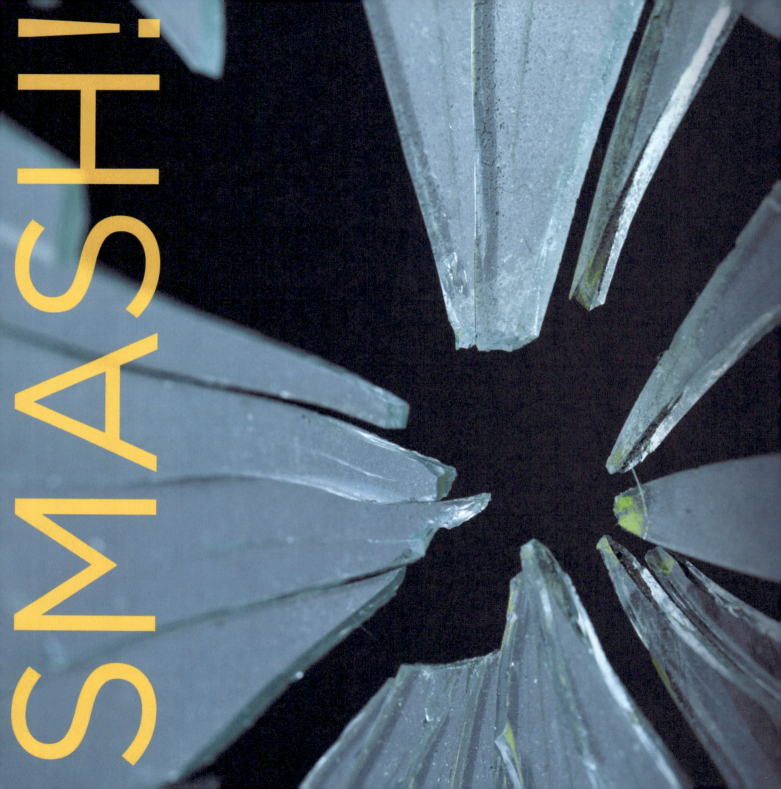

I woke up with my dad next to me crying. I was nine years old and about to hear news that would shape the rest of my life. The hustle and bustle of the hospital was confusing to me. The pain medications were probably producing cognitive effects but I remembered flashes of struggling to move or even walk. I tried to focus on the only thing that was familiar and that was my dad. He looked at me, and I could see that something was very wrong.

"Jon, We were in an accident. You're hurt pretty bad but they think you will be ok"

I said, "I can't move… and where are… Mom and Mark?"

"Jon, Mom and Mark were killed in the accident."

I couldn't focus on or really believe what Dad just told me. How could this be true? I had to let it all sink in.

What I remember from that day seems like someone else's movie, not mine - but this is my story. On August 6, 1983, the van rolled over multiple times, I was thrown forward through the windshield, and my father was trapped in the vehicle.

The cause of the accident is still somewhat unclear. My brother was ejected out of his door and the van rolled over him. My mother hit the steering column with extreme force which caused immediate death. I had multiple skull and rib fractures, a compound fracture in my right femur, and too many lacerations and bruises to count. Dad was shaken and in shock but miraculously had no serious injuries.

Years later I would realize just how lucky we both were but while recovering in that hospital, I was a long way from that realization.

The
Only Child

I could not attend the funerals, because I was laid up in a body cast at the local hospital for three months. My friends came nearly every day and we drank milk shakes, watched TV (Different Strokes was my favorite) and played games with my traction device at the end of the bed. (I did not think that was fun.) It was an amazing outpouring of love that Dad and I received. Words cannot describe the appreciation I have for the families and friends that came to our aid in this time of need.

Either my youth or my unwillingness to comprehend the magnitude of losing half my family kept me from the grieving process. I eventually returned home and I chose to sleep in my brother's room. The first night home a lot of people came and my dad stayed in the room until I fell asleep. I am unable to recall very many memories of that time or even before the accident. I remember my friends having fun pushing me in my wheelchair and sometimes even riding on the back while going downhill. The days and months blurred together until my dad decided he was ready to move on.

Like The
Brady Bunch

My dad started a relationship with a wonderful woman named Pam who was our neighbor when I was much younger. The problem now was they lived six hours apart. I recall my father asking me if it was all right that he was dating and I remember being happy for him. Pam had a daughter, Stacy and a son, Scott. Her son was the same age as I was and during visits he and I were inseparable. We did everything together and I wanted to go visit more and more. Stacy, a few years older, was a very compassionate yet strong young woman. We annoyed Stacy with our antics but she was more than tolerant of our behavior. On one visit to Pam's house, we witnessed TV history when MTV showed the Michael Jackson "Thriller" video. It was a big deal at the time because we did not have cable television in our town.

I did not anticipate that the upcoming years would be such a struggle for our family.

The real world set in **and it was no picnic.**

Dad and Pam's connection was obvious and a few short years later they were married. The challenge of blending our two families had begun. Pam, Stacy and Scott moved into our house which was a good start.

I feel terrible about my hurtful words and actions during that time. I wish I could have had the ability to press a PAUSE button when I was a teenager. Like most families with three teenagers, our house always had a crisis somewhere.

I told my stepmom many times, "There's no owner's manual on how to blend families." If there was a known step-by-step process to ensure no failure in family merging, then sharing it with the world would be fantastic.

What!

I was blessed with good athletic ability but also a very short stature, so I had to work harder to stay competitive as I got older. In my sophomore year of high school I became a "gym rat" along with my best buddies. My good friend Todd, who lived a block away, also went to the gym every day. Friends would pick me up, then go to Todd's house to pick him up for our workout. One morning Todd did not show for the pickup time. We went to the gym and then afterward, decided to swing past his house. A cleaning service and a police car were in his driveway. I panicked since we were into a lot of mischief during that time so I was sure that we were being caught for something.

I went home to call some friends to try to find out what was going on. First I tried Todd's house; the police answered, so I hung up. I called a friend whose dad answered the phone and asked me if I had heard the news. He told me Todd had committed suicide.

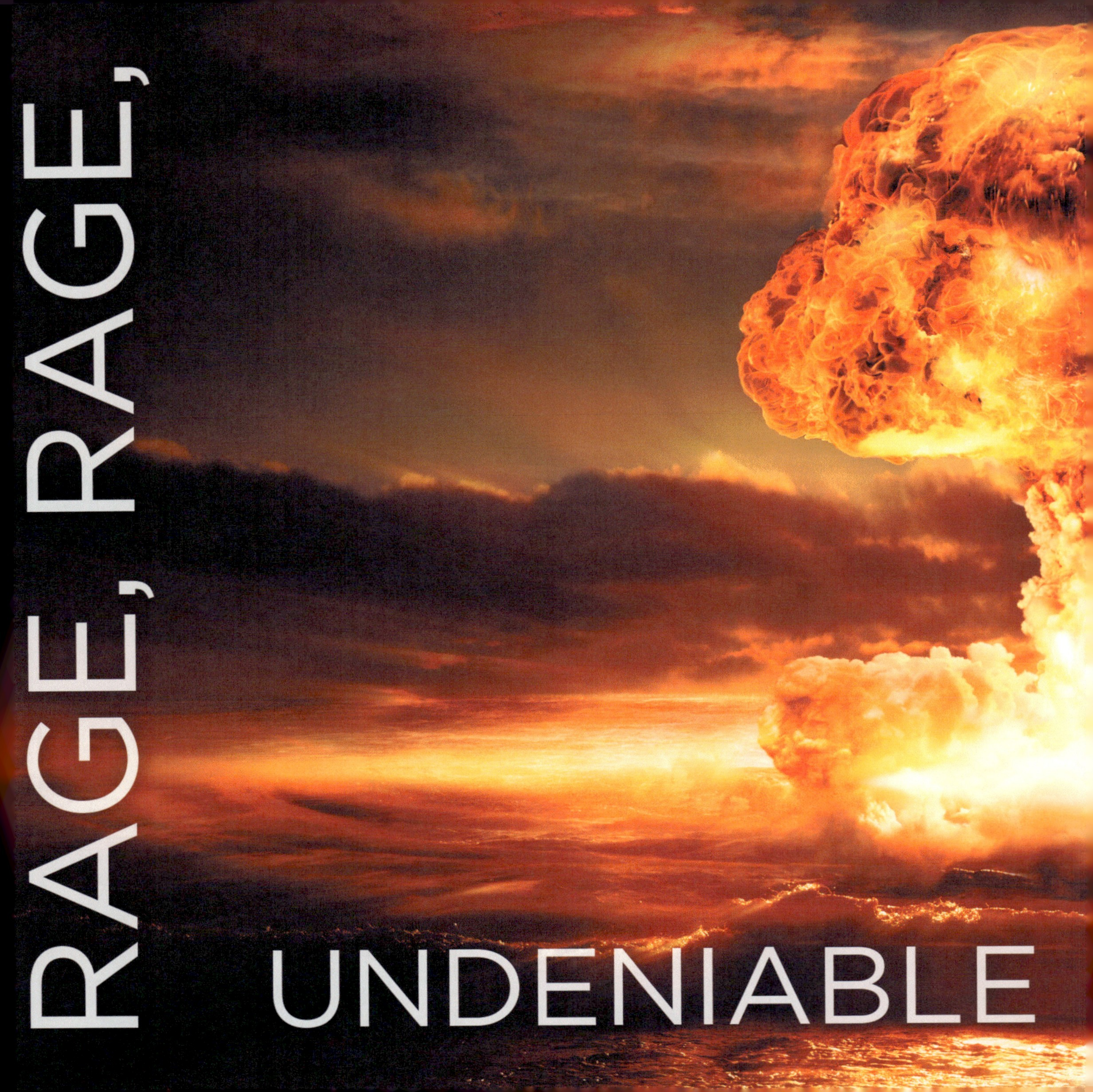
RAGE, RAGE,
UNDENIABLE

RAGE!

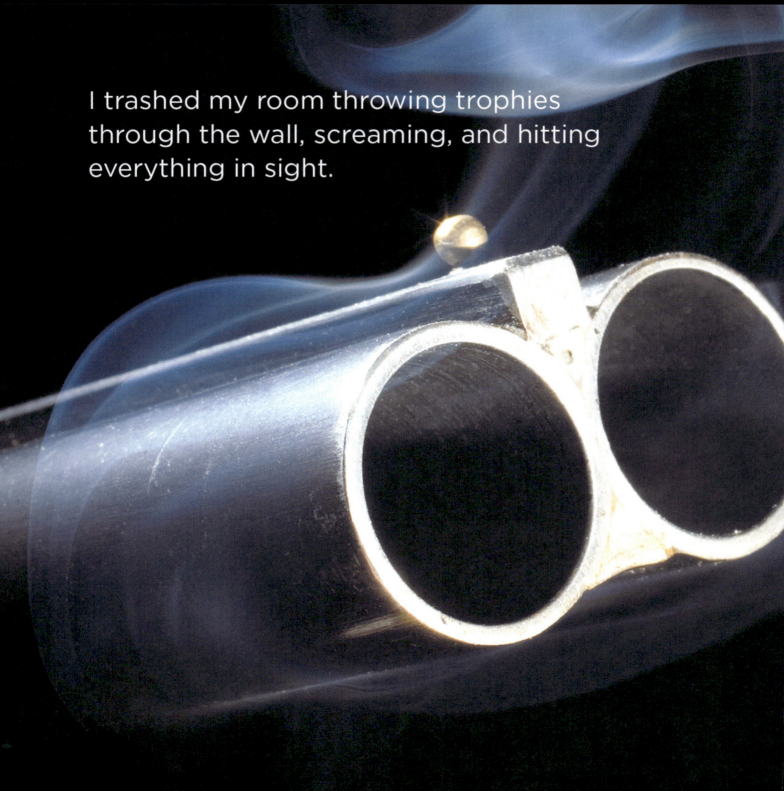

I trashed my room throwing trophies through the wall, screaming, and hitting everything in sight.

I ran outside trying to make sense of the news. The next few days were a blur until we said goodbye to our friend. Todd was buried in the same cemetery as my mother and brother, who were laid to rest only six years prior to Todd's death. I did not visit often. I think I just did my best to deal with these three tragedies by hiding. My hiding eventually included abusing alcohol.

One evening not too long after our friend committed suicide I reached a low point. We were at a friend's house drinking and I found her father's shotgun. I looked at the gun, put the barrel in my mouth, and pulled the trigger. Nothing happened. I fiddled with it and BOOM! The gun went off and shot out a TV. I was terrified and ran outside near our old elementary school until I found the courage to turn myself in to the police.

This would not be the last time I found myself in the custody of law enforcement.

The remainder of the summer and majority of my high school career was a saga of highs and lows.

I always had a conflict between development and self-destruction.

I had many wonderful teachers but my high school government teacher really stands out, not only for teaching us about government but also valuable life lessons. As part of our school work, my fellow classmates and I initiated a bill, which was later passed by our state legislature (LB 922), to recognize influential African Americans in our school history curriculum, especially those who were from our own state.

When I wasn't "saving the world" I was finding a way to feed my addiction. I wasted many days of my life that I won't get back. I was pulled over one night and sent to juvenile hall for driving while intoxicated (DWI). I was too afraid to call my father, so I waited three days in jail. The choice was either rehab or jail. I was fortunate that my father could send me to rehab with the hope this would be the support I needed to get my life back on track. I spent 90 days of my senior year of high school in therapy. It was extremely helpful in providing me avenues to say goodbye to the loved ones I lost. The inability to grieve for previous tragedies was evident and the destructive coping mechanisms I developed were textbook classic. I met some amazing people and realized we all have tragedies and triumphs in life.

In high school I met one of the best people I would ever have the pleasure to call a real friend.

> None of us should take for granted the kind of person who picks you up when you are down, and who doesn't care if you are right or wrong. Cory was with me no matter what, and would give me the shirt off his back if I need it.

He and I had different backgrounds. His dad worked hard on the road driving a truck and my dad was a family dentist. In high school I found the social cliques difficult since I never felt I belonged to one particular group. I didn't understand and still don't understand the point of segregating anyone for any reason. Neither of us cared about who was "in" and who was "out", which was probably why we maintained such a close friendship.

I graduated from high school which is astounding since I don't remember studying at all. I spent more time helping friends who were struggling than I did on my school work. The next step was college and I wanted to become a political lobbyist. I had such a great experience with the state legislature in high school and I was sure that was what I wanted to do. The theory sounded good. But guess what happens when you place

an 18-year-old in an environment full of bad choices, and a lack of good study habits? I had almost completed the fall semester when I decided to drink too much and then get in a car and drive.

The good news was I did not hurt anyone. The bad news – I was in the backseat of a police car and headed back to the courtroom.

The judge gave me a choice, either three years of probation or a month in jail. Thirty days in jail? That's easy, right? I thought it was the better option of the two, because it was quicker and I would not have a monthly meeting with a probation officer. I thought that the chances of my getting in trouble again were high, and I did not want to get charged with probation violation on top of whatever else I did next time. Jail was an interesting culture and I found myself in the awkward position of not fitting into a particular group. I played basketball the first day and got into a fight which is the norm for "fresh meat". I played dominos with one group, read poetry with another guy, and shared my love of sports with anyone who wanted to listen. Jail is not a place you want to be but it did allow me to think about my life and understand my internal resolve. I also learned humans can be wicked and crafty.

I was released, returned to college but did not apply myself or study very well. I wasted my time and family's money that first year of college. It was a hard conversation to have with my parents explaining my failure in school when I knew the problem was me. My parents suggested a career in healthcare. I had already disappointed them almost to the point of no return so I transferred to a community college to take care of prerequisite courses. I have always loved people and admired those who care for the sick, so healthcare was appealing to me.

It's amazing! When I studied, I received good grades and felt like I had accomplished something too. I was finally on the right track. I applied to a radiology tech program and was accepted; and everything started moving forward positively in my life.

"I have always loved people and admired those who care for the sick, so healthcare was appealing to me."

Then, tragedy struck again. I received a chilling phone call. **"Cory has been in a motorcycle accident and is in a coma."** The next month was another blur of doctors, nurses, family members, and worry as Cory drifted into eternal sleep on May 4, 1994. I never built up enough courage to go into the ICU to say goodbye to my friend Cory, and I should have.

Wilhelm Conrad Roentgen

The title of this section pays homage to the man who discovered electromagnetic radiation in a wavelength range known as X-rays. I moved to Sioux City, Iowa to enroll in a hospital-based program for radiologic technology. I was hooked from the first day, and it wasn't because radiology was intriguing, even though I like the science. It was because I was helping people. I still remember how nervous I was the first time I pressed that button. It was a grueling program not affiliated with an academic institution. The students were part of a hands-on, hospital, workforce. I was getting straight A's and knew this time, my life was on track.

As the final year of the program began, I was perfecting my skills and branching out into specialty areas. Late in the evening in fall/winter of 1995 I felt pain in my chest that was different from any pain I had felt before. The next day the doctor's diagnosis was strained muscles. However, I had worked out most of my adult life, and I was familiar with muscle strains. It didn't feel like a strain. I went to bed that evening in a sweat and discomfort. I thought maybe I'd be all right in the morning. Suddenly, I opened my eyes and looked around, but I couldn't breathe. It felt like an elephant was sitting on my chest. I didn't want to call an ambulance at age 21 so I drove myself to the ER. I still can't believe I made it there. I remember parking the car and then falling through the door of the emergency room. The lab tests showed I'd had a heart attack!

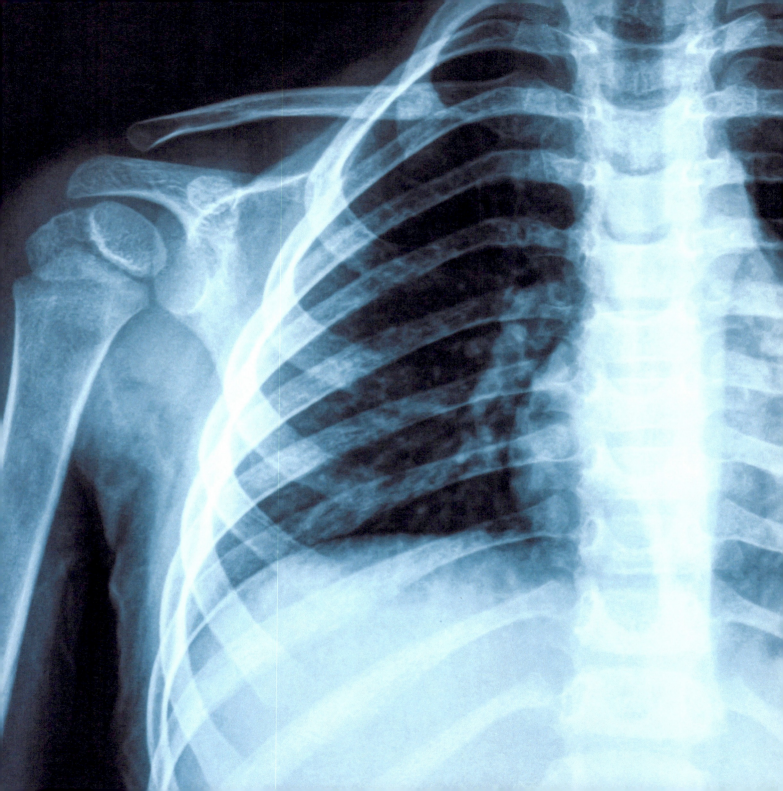

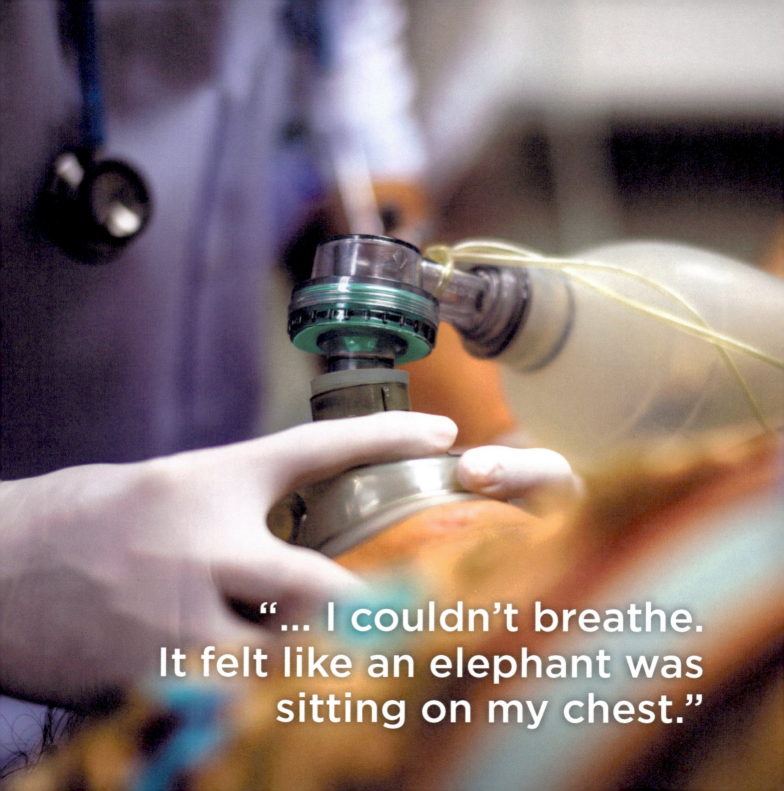

"... I couldn't breathe. It felt like an elephant was sitting on my chest."

I was so uncomfortable and the pain had still not subsided. I knew part of the problem was that I was overweight, smoking, drinking, and had not been to a gym for over a year.

A cardiologist was called in and he was not convinced that I had suffered a heart attack. He ordered a special test to look at the blood vessels of my heart. The test results were good; there were no blockages, yet he still wanted to run more tests. After being in the ICU for a while I was finally diagnosed with myocarditis, an infection of the heart muscle which can be treated, but the muscle cannot be repaired.

A déjà vu moment happened. My dad was again standing next to me while I lay in a hospital bed. I thought, well we have done this before and survived, so why can't we do it again? The next few months were a tough road to recovery. I got better, but I wasn't able to attend my clinical work, so I was falling behind in learning with my fellow students. The next semester I worked even harder making up the hours I missed, and graduated with my peers.

I had tasted some academic success and I knew my dad wanted me to obtain a college degree. I owed it to him to get this accomplished. In 1998 I graduated from the University of Nebraska Medical Center, with a degree in Radiation Sciences, and I heard my dad stand up and cheer. It was one of the best moments in my life to look into the crowd and see my family so proud.

The Young Professional:

I spent the remainder of my 20's working hard and probably partying even harder. I was making money, had great friends, and was experiencing all things in life. The big difference between my friends' partying and my partying was that I thought I needed it to survive. At this time I didn't understand the dependence I had on alcohol, and I can say there were not too many days I went without drinking.

In my mid-20's I took a position as a traveling contractor for radiology services. The money was phenomenal, but for someone with an addiction this was not a good idea. I did my job well no matter where I went, I never missed work, and I traveled across the country experiencing every type of healthcare setting we have in this country. When I was done with work I was alone and away from home which fueled my drinking.

One contract led me to a beautiful town in northeastern Wisconsin. I had a great experience there and the contract was extended several times. I was offered tickets to a football game and tailgate bus to a pretty famous team in the region: The Green Bay Packers. On the bus, I looked up and I saw her. The feeling is indescribable but you know when you know. I didn't know who she was but I knew we were destined to be together.

While working in Green Bay, the physician group asked me if I would like to run their day-to-day operations and learn to perform minor procedures to assist the group. I accepted the position and even convinced the group to send me to a physician extender school so I would be board certified. The first year was terrific. And that girl I met at the game? The woman of my dreams said "Yes" to marry me. I felt truly blessed and I thought she must be a little crazy to marry me.

Life was great and
I finally had it together.
Right?

I finished the extra schooling program and passed the national registry but the physician extender profession had not become fully recognized on a national level. The medical executive committee decided not to grant me privileges. I had a choice to stay and manage the group or look for employment in my new field. Depression set in and I struggled because my wife and I wanted to stay where we were in Green Bay, but the job was not there. I worked so hard in school and I loved helping others, but I felt like my career was going backwards.

One night I was drinking rather heavily, and I decided everyone would be better off if I was no longer around, so I grabbed an extension cord, made a noose, stepped up on a chair, and just as I was making an attempt to hang myself, Amy opened the garage door.

"What are you doing?" she yelled.

It's a great question and I made up some ridiculous answer which she was accustomed to at this point. I stopped what I was doing and went to bed. Again, an angel was looking over me.

The Rollercoaster

The next morning I said I was going to find a job in my new profession. A month later I was offered a job by a company in Georgia and we decided follow this adventure. It was very difficult to leave friends and family up north but my folks had retired to Florida and I had an aunt and uncle in Alabama. The culture was different and exciting to me. I was covering two small rural hospitals and was practicing in a profession that I was proud of and enjoyed.

The winter was strange without snow but we had the greatest news. I came home from work and Amy, who is good with crafts, had made me a card which said she was pregnant. I could not have been happier and, believe me, I told everyone I knew. This was it, my life was really coming together, and I was going to be a father.

My stepmom called and said, "Your dad is not feeling well and is having some tests".

She was not the best at relaying health information, so I asked if I could see the scans. One day I received the envelope. I went into work, popped the disk into my work station and saw what my dad had going on. The rough part about medical knowledge is facing truths, as difficult as they may be. I knew right away my father's cirrhosis of his liver was extremely advanced and his brain had deteriorated as well. I broke down in tears knowing that this was probably the last year of my dad's life.

My stepmom, God bless her, did her best to deal with the situation. She tried to explain that the disease was from a parasite he picked up on vacation. This was partially true, but the parasite did not cause this damage; it was alcohol. The next few months as we were preparing for the baby, my dad got progressively worse. Amy and I tried to do our best by "bubble wrapping" the world and moving ahead with our lives anyway.

We found out we were having a boy and I was so excited, because I was the last generation to carry our family name. I gave my dad the coolest father's day gift I could think of. I arranged to for him to perform the ultrasound on his grandson. It was a very meaningful moment for both of us, and the closest he would get to meeting his grandson. Two months later, on August 17, 2007, our son was born. We called to share the news with everyone. Unfortunately, my dad was already in the hospital and unable to talk.

The next week was strange as I was trying to learn how to take care of a baby, work, and keep track of my father's health. We were lucky to have Amy's tremendous parents come to help us. I called my stepmom and asked if I should come to visit. She said you can if you want, but she wanted me to feel that it was ok if I stayed home with my son. I felt like I needed to go for some reason.

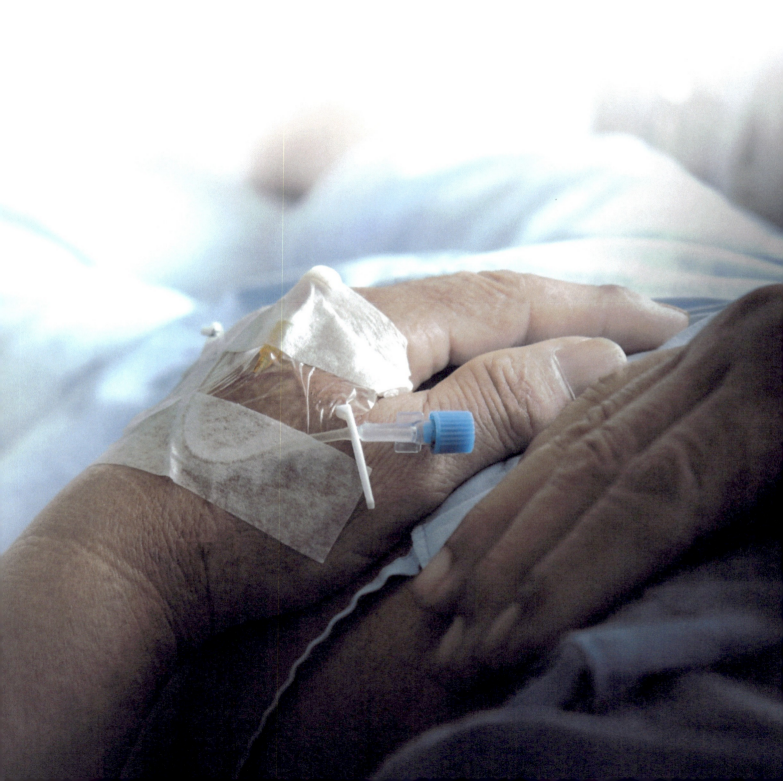

"Strange emotions run through your mind and body as you witness someone you love struggling to breathe."

On September 8, 2007, I arrived at my father's hospice facility. I entered his room and heard his labored breathing. He was unconscious and on comfort measures. The hospice provider came in to check on him.

We asked, "How long do you think it will be?"

Strange emotions run through your mind and body as you witness someone you love struggling to breathe. I didn't want to say goodbye to my dad, but I did want his suffering to be over. Fortunately, we had a distraction. Our favorite college football team was playing, and I watched the game. Our team won and I was able to share that with my dad. The day was ending, and my stepmom and I thought it was time to leave and get some rest.

I couldn't help but think , this might have been how he felt looking over me as I lay in a hospital bed. I grabbed his hand, gave him hug, kissed his forehead and said, "We won the game! I think it's time to go now. I love you!" My stepmom reached over to kiss him, grabbed my hand, and with tears rolling down my dad's face, he gave his last breath. He was only 61.

Being with my dad at his death was a powerful moment that I will never forget and I thank God every day that I drove down to be with him that Saturday morning.

The Tyrant

I continued to work very hard at my job. Shortly after the passing of my father, my boss, who was a very demanding person started yelling at me when I was trying to be in two places at one time. I had been working 60-70 hours a week, so finally I had enough and sent him a message about the importance of treating people with respect. My message angered him to a point where I was eventually terminated. Usually when I tell this story someone asks, "Why did you go to work for him?" Well, this man was a salesman through and through and I was pulled in by his persuasion. There were serious problems in the company and it began to unravel after I left. I felt badly for those who were still employed, especially when the government came in and started asking questions. My former boss was engaging in some illegal actions, was eventually convicted and sent to jail. I had never been fired before but this turned out to be a blessing.

Self-Destructive Routine

We moved back to Wisconsin and my brother-in-law (a fantastic individual) opened his doors to us as we were trying to sell a house in Georgia and find new jobs. Amy was employed right away at her old employer but I was not as fortunate. I fell into a routine of behavior that can only be described as an alcoholic in denial. I was still a responsible father, but since the baby was a pretty good sleeper, I found myself drinking when he went down for a nap. I watched my father for years perform as a high functioning alcoholic, and I was falling into his same footsteps.

I could not live without a drink. It was truly an addiction, but if you asked me at the time, I would say I was fine. "I can control it" but I was just kidding myself, and convincingly too. I was offered a job working nights at a hospital performing radiology exams. My professional career just went backwards about 10 years. I made a great friend working the night shift, and he told me about his brother serving overseas. I wondered, why didn't I ever serve in the military?

GI Jon

What do people do at the beginning of a mid-life crisis? Join the Army. Right? I came home one day and mentioned to my wife that I really wanted to look into serving. She was very supportive and to be honest, I was shocked and excited. I went to visit the recruiter and he said, "You are at the cut off age of 35 so if you don't do it now, it won't happen." The process was much more elaborate than signing your name. I had to gather court records from my previous dealings with law enforcement, write essays, have psychological evaluations, and complete many other tasks. At any time I could have said it wasn't meant to be, but I am a bulldog when faced with adversity. It took five trips to the Military Entrance Processing Station (MEPS) but I was finally awarded the stamp of approval. I would need to leave my wife and two-year-old son plus we also learned Amy was pregnant again.

I was concerned about entering basic training at my age when the average age was 18-22 years old. The physical fitness part wasn't my biggest concern, but rather, how was I going to deal with not drinking or smoking for 11 weeks? I arrived and within two minutes I was doing pushups because I didn't know the commands the drill Sergeant was yelling. What did I get myself into? The first week was a whole lot of poking and prodding. I was not ready for my new reality but everyone else was in the same boat. Surprisingly the age gap was not really a factor except for all the *Grandpa* references. I really got along with these young men and learned WHY I was there.

Armed services is the last chance for some individuals. I don't say that to be dramatic but it is a fact. The upbringing and home environments that some of my fellow soldiers had is hard for most people to comprehend. If they do not succeed in the service, they have a higher percentage of becoming an unfortunate statistic when they return home. I thought I had joined to be a role model for family and get my life straightened out, but I discovered that serving others gave me real fulfillment. The culmination of basic training was another step toward more success.

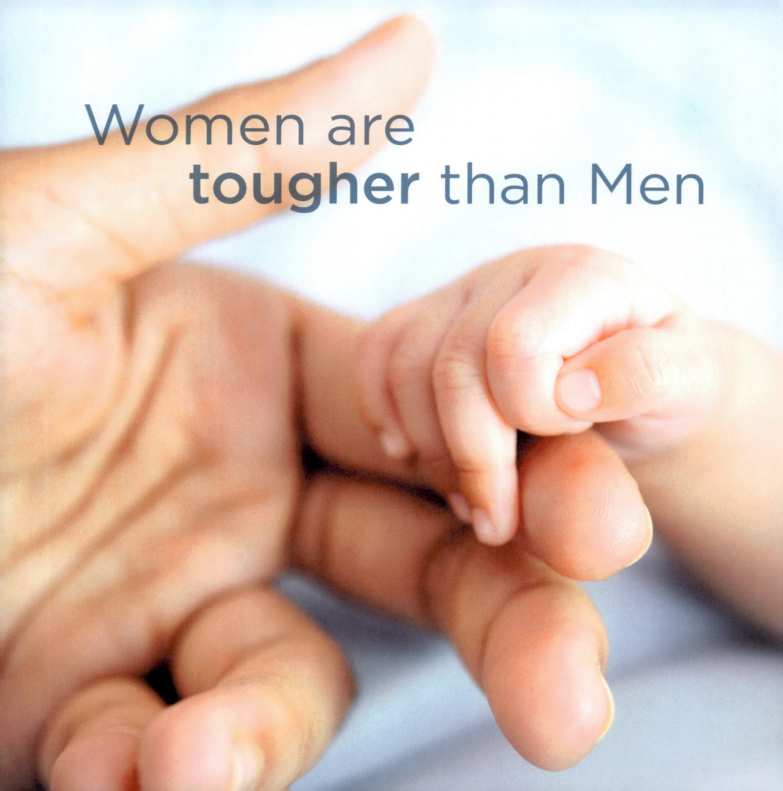

Women are **tougher** than Men

My wife sent me a card during basic training notifying me that we are going to have another boy. She made the card pink to trick me. I was so excited when I returned home. I had kicked the smoking habit and did not run to pick up a drink. I had not yet kicked my addiction, but I was getting close. I had a few beers on a couple of occasions but it didn't give me the same feeling. I was still working the night shift, and I wanted to be present for my second child's birth, so I postponed additional Army training until the winter.

On August 14, 2010, I got off my night shift and arrived home about 7:30 a.m. I noticed that Amy was feeling uncomfortable, but she sent me to bed anyway. At 10:30 a.m. my son ran into the room and said "Mommy told me to tell you it is time to go to the hospital".

I jumped up, got dressed and she said, "Take a shower. We have time". Ok, well, I guess my personal hygiene is more important, so I will do as she asks. The drive to the hospital was only about 10-15 minutes. We called my sister-in-law to meet us at the hospital to take our oldest. We arrived and when I offered Amy a wheelchair and she said , "No, I can walk". A few minutes later we were in the birthing suite, the nurse checked her and said, "Oh boy, please don't push". I looked over and Amy was sweating and in discomfort so I knew we were getting close. There was not time for any "magic medicine" and within a minute of the physician arriving in the room our second child was born. I can't imagine the pain and even though I learned some new combinations of profanity that day I can say with all confidence that men should never complain about pain.

The winter of 2011 I attended accelerated Officer Candidate School. It was only 57 days long, however it was tough. The average night's sleep was about four hours, maybe less if you're in a leadership role. I will not divulge any secrets as those experiences are for fellow candidates and Cadre. What I can say is that I learned valuable lessons about myself. The only outside contact we could have was by postal mail. I corresponded with friends and loved ones as much as I could and distinctly remember being in the laundry room thinking, **"How did I get to this point?"**

I wrote a letter to my buddy, who I worked the night shift with, stating I don't think I am going to drink anymore. I am sure at the time he probably thought I was kidding but I wasn't. Let me be clear that I have no problem with anyone who drinks, but as I took inventory of my self-induced troubles over the past years, the common denominator was alcohol. I think this epiphany was my way of admitting to my addiction. I did not want my wife and children to experience what I had in my father's hospice room.

The two months passed and approximately 50 percent of us made it through OCS and would be commissioned as officers in the Army. I was most excited about coming home and seeing if I could follow through with my commitment to a clean lifestyle.

The FOG has Lifted

Twenty-seven years had passed since my father delivered the heart wrenching news of the passing of my mother and brother in the emergency room in Virginia. Since that time I did not think of them except when I was feeling sorry for myself. Suddenly memories of my early childhood flooded my mind. I am not sure what was fact or fiction since I do not have anyone to ask, but that makes it even more fun so I can pick the good memories. Repressed memories can be scary. However, it is a blessing to know more than what is in a photo album.

My civilian and military life was working well. I had a beautiful wife, two great boys, a good job and wonderful friends. Yet, something was still missing in my life and I had a burning feeling inside that I could do more. I thought about the years I had wasted in a self-destructive spiral. One morning I came into work and one of my colleagues was looking at the internal job postings.

She said, "I think you would be good at that."

"What job are you talking about?"

The job was for a customer service coach. My first thought was, why do we need this in healthcare – everyone should be customer friendly (but I know that is not true from my experience).

I decided to apply and six interviews later I was offered the position from a man who would truly alter my career path. The job was less money, probably more hours and I had no formal education in customer service. I had already taken a step backward in my career and I certainly wouldn't do it again. Right? Yet, I decided the challenge was exciting and accepted the offer. I received so much more than a wage from this job. I discovered people could relate to my life experience and I had a gift for connecting with people.

A sincere heartfelt
"Thank You"
to Eric...

... for taking a chance on me and being one of the most influential mentors in my life.

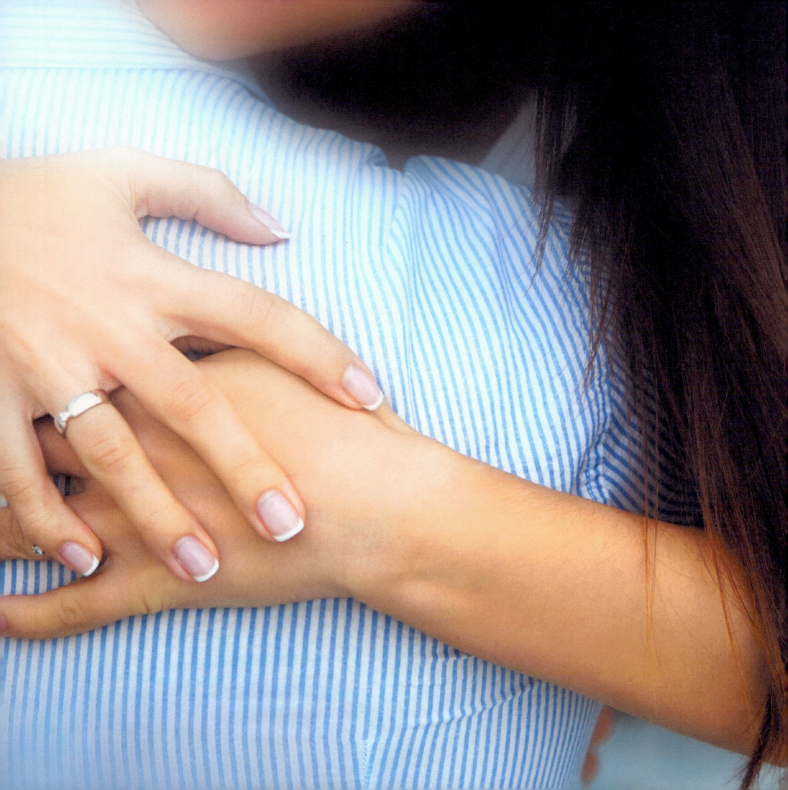

Lessons Learned

"Start by doing what is necessary, then do what's possible, suddenly you are doing the impossible." — *St. Francis of Assisi*

Why would I share so much about myself? I learned I am not alone; there are others out there with challenging stories. Through sharing our stories, we can help each other. I remember darker days, negative thoughts, and feelings of hopelessness. Now, I've realized it's possible to do what I thought was impossible – by changing the direction of my life. I developed these five actions that have helped me make positive changes.

Thrive with Five

1. **Decide**: As much as I would like to give you a magic pill to make the obstacle, challenge or pain go away, I can't. You are the only one who can make the change. It's your choice. Make the decision to change your life.

2. **Commit to Action**: Don't wait until tomorrow. You can stop the hurting, right now—today. No one is stopping you from living the life you want. Write down what you want, tell people your plan, and face the challenge.

3. **Partnership**: Surround yourself with people who support your decision. You cannot do it alone. As hard as it may be, let go of friendships, habits or even employment that is hurting you. This is a necessary step.

4. **Make a checklist for Improvement:** Make an inventory of your life (good and bad) and never stop working on yourself.

5. **Love**: If you fail to love, you will never know true happiness.

It is **scary** jumping into the unknown

DECIDE

Deciding to make a life change is the hardest step. The majority of people will not decide to change because it feels uncomfortable. Change can be hard because of withdrawal from an addiction, staying in an unhappy job just for the paycheck, maintaining an unhealthy relationship or other reasons, because we are afraid to let go. You will come up with every excuse NOT to make a positive decision. Your internal struggle ultimately fuels success or failure. It is easy to wallow in self-pity and say **WHY ME?** But what you should be asking is **WHY NOT ME!**

but the reward is worth the anxiety.

The biggest step is to **DECIDE:** "I want my life to be like _____". Think about it and you will know the answer.

#2 COMMITMENT TO ACTION

Commit to your decision and plan of action.

The plan has been in your brain for long time. **Just START!** The first action is to get up in the morning. Yes, that simple act demonstrates you have a passion for life which is a huge motivating factor. There will be stumbles, ups and downs, pressures, and physical and mental pain. You will even doubt yourself sometimes, but remember the commitment you made and honor it. The successes may be small at first, but celebrate each one and commit to the next part of your plan. Let's say you want to earn a college degree. One class will not get you there but one at a time will. The journey may be long or short, but know that every stage has its own successes. Once you feel success, you will want to maintain that positive momentum in every facet of your life. Make your actions realistic to the challenge ahead and know that there is no quick fix. Develop a personal routine that ends with you saying; "Life is too short not to act", then you are on the right path. The action must be observable and measureable. This means you will need to be able to see or feel the result of the action. The action plans may grow and change over time, but your routine can adapt to any situation.

PARTNERSHIP

Together we can make it happen. I have learned that I need others to help me reach my goals. I began running a few years ago, partially because Uncle Sam said so, but really as a way for me to be with my thoughts. My wife inspired me to run a marathon and now I have completed four, 26-mile marathons. Running is an individual sport but without support from family and friends I would never have accomplished this goal.

Surround yourself with people who believe what you believe in.

I was introduced to the phrase "Teamwork Makes the Dream Work" by an Army instructor and it wasn't until a year later when I read John C. Maxwell's book, *Teamwork Makes the Dream Work* that I knew where this quote came from and now my family has made it our motto. I highly recommend the book.

Work on improving every day.

You are living for a purpose and you do matter. If you have found that purpose I congratulate you, and if you have not, that is OK. The key factor for this action is improvement whether you know exactly what you want to do or not. You will never reach perfection. I realize that is a shock, but striving to be your best is good enough. As long as you make continual effort to get better, you are successful. Read books, exercise more, meet new people, renew your faith, continue your education, or take up a new hobby, and you will find that this thing called life is a fun ride. The possibilities are only limited by your imagination.

List events in your life and revisit those trials, tribulations and triumphs. Remember what got you to this point. Take responsibility for your behavior. Improving yourself is a continuous process, and for me it was very difficult at first, but with time it got better. Trust me. Regret can consume you and lead to failure. Forgive yourself and make today better for someone else. Life is about experiences both good and bad. I have learned my happiest days are when I am helping someone else. Before you know it, your life that was once filled with dark memories or doubt will be replaced with positive thoughts and behaviors that fuel continual success.

The "L" word is often used in connection with material possessions or things. **I challenge you to love yourself,** love what you do and love the people around you. How can you love anything else if you don't first love yourself? I still struggle with my life every day – trying to lose weight, avoiding alcohol, keeping my relationships healthy and doing well in my job.

First, decide to love yourself. Second, love what you do. I see too many people working in jobs that make them unhappy. It isn't about the money. If you love what you're doing you will find that fulfillment is better than all the things you can buy. How do you know if you love something? Are you willing to do everything in your power to keep it? Here is my example: I LOVE PEOPLE. I will do everything in my power to continue to teach people how to communicate, connect with each other, motivate those around them and inspire all of us to be better people. Third, love is what you give to another person. This does not mean being intimate. The challenge is putting yourself out there before others, which makes you vulnerable. This challenge is the reason we put up barriers, or walls, so we can feel safe. Take a risk and love someone. Of course, there is a chance of being hurt, but give it a chance. When you think about it, the riskiest thing anyone does is life itself. You already know the eventual outcome. **The love you give and receive is worth any heartache.**

A smile is a terrible

These five actions work only if you are willing to start. It has worked for me and I know it can work for you no matter what the challenge. Success can be defined in many ways but I think **success is what you accomplish after what is expected.**

Right now say out loud: The next time I am faced with a difficult challenge I will change my thought process from **WHY ME?** to **WHY NOT ME!** As I stated earlier, I have always had an internal drive either for self-development or self-destruction. I now choose development of myself and those around me.

I appreciate your taking time to read my story. Life is a great adventure. Laugh, cry, shout, meditate, pray or do whatever you need to make your day truly outstanding for yourself and those around you.

thing to waste. Pass it on.☺

Thank you

Dixie, Howard, and Scott Lederer - Todd's Family

Roger, Brandt, and Colby Olson - Cory's Family

Jim Kubik - Government Teacher in High School

Eric Dordel - Best Boss anyone could every ask for.

Annette Grunseth - Copy Editing

Robb and Michelle without whom this project may never have been completed. You are an amazing team with a true gift and I could not do this without you.

All current and former men and women of our Armed Forces

Speaking Engagements

Author Jon A. Logan is an energetic and engaging speaker, trainer, and coach. He is passionate about helping people to reach their full potential in every aspect of life.

Each toolbox is unique to every organization or individual. To learn more or book a speaking engagement visit www.motivationinnovation.com/motivate or use the QR code below.